PRAYING THROUGH AFFLICTION

Little Morsels of Hope

By
Shareese Britton-Ahorlu

All scripture taken from:

http://www.lockman.org New King James Version (NKJV). Copyright © 1982. Thomas Nelson.

New International Version (NIV). Copyright © 1973, 1978, 1984, 2011 by Biblica, Inc.

Dedication

To my husband, children and family; God truly blessed me when He chose each one of you to walk beside me on this journey called life. Words cannot encapsulate the love and gratitude I have for all of you. To my dear readers, who may feel that life has exacerbated you, even to the point of hopelessness; I pray that you find peace and tiny morsels of hope within the pages of this book.

CONTENTS

Introduction

What if I told you, devoting yourself to your God-given gifts and perseverance through the storms and trials of life; with faith will not only bring fulfillment, but will strengthen you to impact the lives of everyone you encounter. In this moment you may not feel like the fearfully and wonderfully created child of God that you are. However, I assure you, after reading the pages of this book of hope; filled with prayers, testimonies and devotion, purpose will begin to explode on the inside of you. My prayer is that the Holy Spirit living inside of you will ignite and activate your inherent gifts. Come, take this journey with me, as we navigate through this book of hope. Let's discover the power that is buried deep within; the power that you are unaware of. You have not stumbled upon this book by chance. Do not lose hope. Do not despair. Please do not give up! I know you're tired. You may feel abandoned and defeated, but your prosperous future is only a few moments away. Persevere!

Hope

Grace and peace. Webster's dictionary defines hope as "a desire accompanied by expectation of, or belief in fulfillment". My prayer for you today is that you would never give up hope, or the expectation that God can move mightily in your life. God is faithful to His promises concerning you as it is written in

Deuteronomy 7:9 NKJV *"therefore know that the Lord your God, he is God, the faithful God who keeps covenant and mercy for a thousand generations with those who love him and keep his commandments."* God's promise is that our days to come, also known as our future, will be greater than anything we could have experienced in our past. **Job 8:7 NKJV** states *"Though your beginning was small, yet your latter end would increase abundantly.".* Maybe things did not manifest in the way you envisioned, but that does not mean you have to lament and live in despair! It's important, more importantly vital, to trust God even in our painful moments. It is written in **Psalm 62:8 NKJV** *"Trust in Him at all times you people; pour out your heart before Him; God is a refuge for us!"* Therefore, pour out your concerns as well as your disappointments to God, He will comfort you and remind you that He has a plan for your life. It is time to let go of the old and boldly launch into the new season of life that God has prepared for you! Blessings.

Faith

Grace and peace. The recent events that have been occurring throughout the world has caused fear, panic, division, and despair across the various sectors of life. I am not sure if you have noticed, but there has been a spiritual shift and a call for the people of God to guard their hearts from death gripping fear, in order to allow God's peace to rest upon them. If you stay in the presence of the Lord, fear or demonic spirits cannot harm you! God has not given permission for you to be tormented by fear, panic, or despair. Instead, it is written in **2 Timothy 1:7** He has given you *"power love and a sound mind."* Every obstacle you face in this season is Satan's final attempt to prevent you from walking in purpose. You must remember to trust God, activate your faith, and know that even in the middle of the storm, He is in the boat with you! Consequently, let your FAITH be Bigger than your fear and may God's kingdom come and will be done in your life as it is in heaven. Amen

Scriptures for Meditation

Philippians 4:8 NIV *"Finally, brothers and sisters, whatever is true, whatever is noble, whatever is right, whatever is pure, whatever is lovely, whatever is admirable--if anything is excellent or praiseworthy--think about such things. Whatever you have learned or received or heard from me or seen in me-put it into practice. And the God of peace will be with you."*

Philippians 4:5-7 NIV *"Rejoice! 5 Let your gentleness be evident to all. The Lord is near. 6 Do not be anxious about anything, but in every situation, by prayer and petition, with thanksgiving, present your requests to God. 7 And the peace of God, which transcends all understanding, will guard your hearts and your minds in Christ Jesus."*

Matthew 8:23-26 NIV *"Then he got into the boat and his disciples followed him. 24 Suddenly a furious storm came up on the lake, so that the waves swept over the boat. But Jesus was sleeping. 25 The disciples went and woke him, saying, "Lord, save us! We are going to drown!" 26 He replied, "You of little faith, why are you so afraid?" Then he got up and rebuked the winds and the waves, and it was completely calm."*

<u>Love Never Fails</u>

Greetings. Many people ask couples what the secret is to a long-lasting marriage/ relationship. In fact, there is no secret at all. Each of us have been given instructions on how to be successful at love. It is in a little book called the Bible. We have all heard the acronym …**B**asic **I**nstructions **B**efore **L**eaving **E**arth. There is more truth to this acronym than we know.

Ecclesiastes 4:9-12 NKJV states *"Two are better than one because they have a good reward for their labor for if they fall one will lift up his companion but woe to him who is alone when he falls for, he has no one to help him up again if two lie down together they will keep warm but how can one be warm alone though one may be overpowered by another two can withstand him and the threefold cord is not easily broken."* You may think to yourself; is this referring to a triple braided cord? Triple means three, not two. The most important cord is the first and central cord, which is God. **Luke 12:31NKJV** tells us *"But seek the Kingdom of God and all these things shall be added to you."* If you seek God first and put God first, not only in marriage, but in every relationship in your life…it will not easily be broken. Make God the central cord and love will be added to you; **patience** will be added to you; **kindness** will be added to you; **meekness** will be added to you; **gentleness** will be added to you; **peace** will be added to you; **hope** will be added to you; **true**

forgiveness will be added to you; **perseverance** will be added to you… **a long-lasting fulfilling relationship** will be added to you. We all know we are human and not perfect. Therefore, when we forget and cannot see the evidence of God being that central cord in our relationship…we must remind ourselves that, to have perfect love we must self-reflect and compare our actions to the instructions in **1Corinthians 13:4-8 NIV** which states *"Love is patient. Love is kind. It does not envy. It does not boast. It is not proud. It is not rude. It is not self-seeking. It is not easily angered. It keeps no record of wrongs. Love does not delight in evil but rejoices with the truth. It always protects, always trust, always helps, always perseveres. Love never fails."* When we follow these basic God given instructions in all our relationships, there is nothing we cannot conquer together, because again love never fails.

Prayer ONE

God, I come before You now, with the spirit of thankfulness in the middle of this storm. I know who You are. I know Your character. I trust that You know the plans that You have for me. They are plans to make me prosper and not to harm me, to give me your hope and the future You ordained. As I go through these trials and tribulations of life, God help me to remember Your character. Help me to remember exactly Who You are. Help me to remember God, that You are faithful to Your promises concerning me. I know that I can always come to Your altar and leave anything that concerns me. All my problems, all my burdens, all my worries. I can hand them over to You at this altar, so You can carry them. You told me in Your word that when I am tired, I should come unto You when I am weary and heavy laden and You will give me rest; take Your yoke upon me and learn of You because Your yoke is easy Your burden is light (Matthew 11:28-30). Therefore, I come to do as instructed, by taking Your yoke upon me. Break every chain and every yoke that is hindering me from moving into my next. Every heavy burden God is for You to carry, and not me. I will focus on today. I will live for today. I refuse to worry about tomorrow. It is written in Your word that I shouldn't worry, for tomorrow has its own worries. You didn't create me to worry, but You created me to worship. Consequently, I worship you now God. I worship in spite of what my flesh feels. I worship in spite of what the circumstances look like. I worship You, because I know who you are. You are the giver of my breath, the giver of life. You have delivered me from the hand of the enemy so many times. That is Your character! No matter what I face, whether it's spiritual, emotional/mental or physical, You are my deliverer. You are the hero, not me. I take my hands off of what You are doing. I give You, my heart. I trust You with my life because You are the architect. You have the blueprints I do not. God, I may not be able to see what You're doing, but I know that Your hand is in it, and it will be good. I may not know what my next step or move is, but I know that You have ordered each step. I thank You and bless You this day in spite of what I'm feeling; in spite of what it looks like; in spite of how the enemy has been trying my very soul. Trusting and worshipping You in spite of. In Jesus name, Amen.

<u>Affliction, Prayer, Hope</u>

My prayer is that God will continue to embrace you through these devotions and that His perfect will is done in your life. **Romans 12:12 NIV** states *"Be joyful in hope, patient in affliction, faithful in prayer."* Webster's dictionary defines affliction as something that causes pain and suffering. There are many areas in our lives where we may experience periods of affliction. Some include, our physical & mental health, finances, children, identity, relationships, marriages/partnerships, career, death of a loved one. **Romans 12:12 NIV** tells us that we have to *be joyful, patient and faithful when we are experiencing pain and suffering...* if we are completely honest with ourselves no one wants to do that. Our first instinct is to flee. King David was afflicted in many ways. He knew exactly who to call out to...the Father. **Psalms 25:16 NIV** David called out to the *Lord "turn to me and be gracious to me, for I am lonely and afflicted. Relieve the troubles of my heart and free me from my anguish. Look upon my affliction and my distress and take away all my sins. See how numerous are my enemies and how fiercely they hate me, guard my life and rescue me, do not let me be put to shame, for I take refuge in you."*

King David knew that his only way out was to lean into the Father, put his faith in God and persevere. Perseverance is defined as the continued effort to do or achieve something despite difficulties failures or opposition, steadfastness. God never promised that we would not have difficulties, failures, affliction, or opposition, but He did promise to

- **never leave or forsake us** (Deuteronomy 31:8)
- **to hide us and give us refuge under his wing** (Psalm 91:4)
- **to give us strength to endure** (Isaiah 41:10)
- **to lift up a standard when the enemy come in like a flood** (Isaiah 59:19)
- **to leave the Holy Spirit to be our comforter and helper** (John 14:26)

Ask yourself, what afflictions do I have? Am I just going to flee or am I going to ask God to activate the Holy Spirit within and persevere? God is our everlasting Father so hold on, press into God and persevere through. The **blessing** is on the other side of the **pressing**.

Prayer:

God, I come before You with a humble heart asking for forgiveness of my sins, that I may be holy and acceptable in your sight. Lord, I bless You and thank You for giving me another day to propel into my purpose and persevere through any affliction or unbearable circumstance in my life. Let Your word be edifying to my soul. Help me to remember that You have placed every tool that I may need within me. I am equipped to face whatever challenge comes my way. Remind me that You are always with me. Activate the Holy Spirit that lives within me to help me to endure this race and I will forever give Your name the Glory and honor it deserves. In Jesus Name, Amen.

Perseverance Through the Darkness

Grace and Peace. My prayer is that our God will continue to encourage you to persevere through the many trials of life, knowing that you are to be a light in the dark places for His Glory.

Meditation Scriptures

Psalm 9:9-10 NIV *"the Lord is a refuge for the oppressed a strong hold in times of trouble, those who know Your name will trust in You for You Lord have never forsaken those who seek you."*

Psalm 27:1 *NIV* *"the Lord is my light and my salvation, whom shall I fear? the Lord is the stronghold of my life, of whom shall I be afraid?"*

Psalm 55:22 NIV *"cast your cares on the Lord and He will sustain you, He will never let the righteous be shaken."*

Our world has become a very dark place, as a result of many abandoning God, to follow after false idols. There seems to be no light in the darkness... There seems to be no end in sight... but those thoughts that your trials will last always are a trick of the enemy. The enemy wants you to believe that God has abandoned you...He wants you to believe that God didn't plant that vision...he wants you to believe that God doesn't hear your prayers... he wants to cut off all communication between you and the divine. If he succeeds in deceiving you, the same miracles that God once performed and can still perform will be aborted in your life. The Holy Spirit wants you to P.P.U.S.H. Persevere in Prayer Until Something Happens. God is your light He is your salvation...He is Who you are to put your trust in; no matter what circumstances you face in your lifetime...He is faithful even when you are not. The trial you are going through now may seem like it will never end. That is a lie from the enemy of our soul...whether it is financial difficulties, hiccups in the startup of your business, persecution at work, challenges and rebellion among your children, lingering sickness, discord and strife in your family relationships...Whatever you are pressing through; you have to remember that you are both the salt and the light of the earth....you are not easily broken ...you must go through the refining process to come out as pure gold ....keep P.P.U.S.H.ING! The blessing is on the other side...the reward is on the other side! God did not equip you with all the gifts that He placed inside of you to not utilize them...God did not leave you with His word, so that you would not stand on it. Today you must ask yourself: am I P.P.U.S.H.ING? (Persevere in Prayer Until Something Happens)

Prayer

God, I thank You for Your word. You said that You would be my refuge, my strength, and my ever present help in trouble... help me to remember Your word to hide it in my heart, that I may not sin against You ... help me God to persevere in prayer until something happens...Help me, not only to pray, but to walk in my purpose, knowing that the world is waiting for me to birth all that You have placed inside of me...I ask God that You would give me the spirit of urgency to do Your will. I pray that You will make my heart and mind malleable to Your will. I know God that I am the salt and the light. Help me to bring that light into the darkness, by the power of the Holy Spirit that resides in me. I will forever give Your name the praise glory and honor that it deserves in Jesus' name Amen.

Perseverance Through Depression

Grace and peace. As promised, I have agreed to share some testimonies in this book of hope, despite being a very private person. When I started writing God reminded me that this is not about me, but all about being a witness for Him. We overcome by the blood of the lamb and by the word of our testimony. Hence, now that I have laid the groundwork for affliction and perseverance, let us reflect on the word of God.

Meditation scriptures

Psalm 30:2 NIV

"Lord my God I called to You for help, and you healed me. You, Lord bought me up from the realm of the dead; You spared me from going down into the pit. Sing the praises of the Lord, you his faithful people; praise His holy name. For His anger lasts only a moment, but His favor lasts a lifetime; weeping may remain for a night, but rejoicing comes in the morning."

Testimony: When I was 18 years old, I was an atheist. I grew up in church, but believed that if there was a God, how could so many dreadful things happen in our world? Why do innocent people suffer? Where is this God that is supposed to be with us? I concluded that religion and the concept of God was a tool used by those in positions of power to rule over the masses. I was not going to be led by blind faith in this God, who I could not see or feel was present. Depression set in after months of living recklessly with no fulfillment. It was during this time that I suffered, what I believed at the precious age of 18, through some of the toughest moments in my life. My parents were getting a divorce. I didn't have money to pay for college after already beginning. I broke up with my high school sweetheart. I was failing in school. I gained weight (the freshman 15) and struggled with my body image. I felt like my life was falling apart. I stopped eating and showering, I began sleeping more throughout the day and did not go to classes, I lost interest in activities, avoided being with my friends, or anyone who would spark joy or hope, because it hurt so much to be happy. It was actually painful to smile. I spent days at a time weeping in bed, until there were no more tears left to cry. I started saying things like, I wonder what it would feel like to go to sleep and never wake up again. I contemplated suicide. After several weeks of this, my college roommate called my mom. My mom came to campus immediately and could not believe the state that I was in. I was very good at hiding how I really felt and she had absolutely no idea what was happening to me. I will always remember her words; she changed my life. She said "I am either bringing you to the hospital now to see a psychiatrist, or I could bring you home and we go to church on Sunday." I had no problem going to see a psychiatrist, because I believed in the power of medicine and psychosocial therapy, but not in this God who I thought did not exist. However, my mom believed more in the power of Jesus. She prayed for me and decided we would try Jesus first. I had no interest in going into a church. I used to tell my family that if I went into the church, it would crumble and fall, because of how much I testified that there was no God. We went to church that Sunday (the building is still standing). I made sure that I sat all the way in the back pew, so as not to draw attention to myself. The pastor began to preach and when he did, it felt as though everyone around me in the church disappeared and it was just, he and I. Pastor Roderick Allen was speaking directly to my soul. In that moment I felt the presence of God and knew He was real. There was no way that this man, that I had never met, could know and speak about the deep parts of me and exactly what I was experiencing; the despair, hopelessness, the feeling of wanting to give up and die. Prior to the service ending, I was on my knees crawling to the altar. God filled me with His Holy Spirit, and I began to speak in a heavenly language. I have been following Him ever since. There is a void in the heart of man toward God and nothing will ever fill it, but Him. Believe me, I tried to find a substitute, but there was none. The spirit of heaviness lifted from me immediately at that altar. I would like to tell you that my life since then has been filled with rainbows and sunshine, but we all know that wouldn't be the truth. There were days when I still persevered through thoughts of depression, by praying and petitioning God. My mind was a battlefield, but with God's word and faith, He helped me persevere. Amen

Prayer:

God, I come before you with a humble and grateful heart. I want to thank you for lifting me out of the pit of despair. I know that if You did it for me you can do it from others. I bind the spirit of depression right now in the name of Jesus and send it to the pit of hell and loose the joy of the Lord which is my strength. There may be someone who is feeling depressed right now...hold on, persevere through...don't give up...He hears your cries... weeping may endure for night, but joy will surely come in the morning. I am living proof! I am the evidence! Pray, Lord I ask that You embrace me and surround me with Your love. Jesus, hide me under your wing and let me know, there is nothing to be ashamed of...You love me. You died for me, You paid the price so I didn't have to. I know nothing is impossible with You and I bless You. I submit myself to Your will and I will forever give Your name the glory that You deserve. In Jesus Name

Prayer TWO

God thank you for this moment. Thank you for continuously being with me and walking me through the different seasons of my life. I pray that you would help me to be obedient to your instructions during this next season of my life. I don't want to be like the children of Israel who roamed in the wilderness for more than 40 years, because they could not follow instructions. Forgive me today, for not following your instructions always. I admit that I have the tendency to procrastinate; making things take longer than necessary, because of my disobedience. I know that when You speak oh God, it's not a suggestion, but a command, to do the things that You have placed before me to accomplish in this lifetime. I know there is somebody waiting on the other end of this prayer and the words of this book, for their deliverance. Who am I to hold that up? I come before you today to pray for the nations, who don't acknowledge you in their ways. Whose paths are not being directed. With all the fear, turmoil, and chaos in the world we need You. We need Your protection. we need Your angels to come and stand guard over our homes. I ask that You saturate my home with the blood of Jesus. Cover it from the top to the foundation, so that no evil will come or try to dwell here. Cleanse my atmosphere of anything that is unlike You. I want my home to be where Your Spirit dwells, not just my physical home, but my body as well. Holy Spirit, I give permission for Your Spirit to dwell here in my home and in my body. Help me to always abide in You, so You can abide in me. Help me to let go of anything that no longer serves me. Make it easy. Help me to cut and sever the ties, so that they cannot keep me bound any longer. You are welcome, come into my life and reign. I trust You. I worship you in the middle. I remember my beginning. I may not know where I am headed, but I trust you because You have given me a promise for my future. I need You in the middle to strengthen me, to hold me up and to increase my faith. Thank you for being with me never leaving or forsaking me in Jesus' name Amen.

Perseverance Through Feelings of Betrayal

My prayer for you is that God would use me to help loosen the shackles that have you bound. As I told you before I am a very private person, but the Spirit of the Lord wants me to expose myself to help impact the world one person at a time. As Christians, we often don't share parts of our journey, for fear of judgment, perception and to protect our image. God reminded me that He did not allow me to persevere through the trials of my life to keep my testimony bottled up, when it could propel someone into their healing. Many see polished goods, but do not know what process the raw material had to go through to get into their current position and posture.

Meditation Scriptures
Colossians 3:12-14 NIV
"Therefore, as God's chosen people, holy and dearly loved, clothe yourselves with compassion, kindness, humility, gentleness and patience; bear with each other and forgive one another; if any of you has a grievance against someone, forgive as the Lord forgave you and over all these virtues, put on love which binds them all together in perfect unity."

I Corinthians 13:4-8 NIV

"Love is patient, love is kind, it does not envy, it does not boast, it is not proud, it is not rude, it is not self-seeking, it is not easily angered, it keeps no record of wrongs, love does not delight in evil, but rejoices with the truth. It always protects, always trusts, always hopes, always perseveres, love never fails..."

Matthew 6:12-14 NIV

"Forgive us our debts, as we also have forgiven our debtors and lead us not into temptation, but deliver us from the evil one, for if you forgive men when they sin against you your heavenly Father will also forgive you, but if you do not forgive men their sins your Father will not forgive your sins."

Testimony:

A few years ago, I contemplated giving up on my marriage. A simple untruth uttered by my beloved husband created feelings of betrayal. One simple untruth made me question everything, causing my imagination to run wild. The thoughts embedded in me were: my marriage was healthy, we loved each other, we enjoyed each other's company, we were intimate, therefore, there was nothing that could come between us. Of course, like any other relationship, we had our disagreements, however, we were always able to forgive each other. Who would have thought that we would be facing a trial like this, at this point in our marriage. In that instant, life felt like it shifted—it was as if everything had turned upside down. I was heartbroken, deceived, and destroyed. I thought I was a wonderful wife, a virtuous woman and my husband's crowned jewel. Why me? After days of turmoil, strife, feelings of inadequacy and questioning God, I prayed like I never prayed before, for wisdom and guidance. God gave me an answer that I didn't want and I didn't care for. Instead, what I wanted to do was rebel and allow pride to rule over my life. I wanted to deliberately disobey the direct instructions of God. I made the decision to no longer work on my marriage. Ah, but the Holy Spirit! The Holy Spirit will cause you to do things that you never thought you'd be able to do...He will allow you to bear things that you thought you would never be able to bear...He will comfort and bring light to you in times of darkness...I heard the Spirit of the Lord tell me to stay and persevere, because He ordained our marriage. It was God's will. God began to show me myself, causing me to meditate on what it means to love like He does **(1Corinth 13:4-8)**. Was this the type of love I exemplified? I was not perfect. I was not as virtuous as I thought; I was and we must all be accountable for our actions and the part we play in our circumstances. My mind literally became a daily battlefield. I encountered spiritual warfare like never before. I had to stand on God's word, have faith and trust Him, like I never trusted Him before. God is truly with us when we go through the refining process. God orchestrated a divine chance encounter with a woman named Pastor Luciela. She was serving as a mentor for Daughters of Zion Women of Destiny Ministry. I did not know her, but she asked if she could pray for me. I understood that God was setting me up. As she prayed for me, I literally felt the chains being broken off...All she said was you have to forgive whoever betrayed you, in order to be free. God will fix it and you will never be in this circumstance again. God used her as His mouthpiece, to confirm what He already told me...God had already told me to forgive, be intentional, put the work in and keep praying...He would make my marriage better than it had ever been. He was going to give us that **1 Corinthians 13:4-8** love...He had to prune it to make it grow, then crush it to produce wine. I have truly learned the power of forgiveness and I am so thankful that I was obedient to God. We persevered and God has blessed us abundantly. Not only in our marriage, but in every area of our lives, and the fruit of our labor is evident to all those who have watched us grow through the process. Amen

Prayer

God, I come before You with a humble heart, with praise and thanksgiving. I bless You for being a good Father, for hiding me under Your wing, for overshadowing me when I go through the trials of life. I thank you for sending Your Holy Spirit to comfort

me and to walk with me through the valley of the shadow of death. I pray right now Lord, for anyone who may be experiencing feelings of inadequacy, loneliness, emptiness, anyone going through spiritual warfare in their minds. I pray for those of us who may be contemplating fleeing, when You told them to fight. If it is Your will that I persevere to preserve what you have ordained, help me to obey Your instructions. Help me to forgive as you forgave me. Help me to have the courage and will to overcome betrayal in every area of my life. In Jesus name Amen

Perseverance Through Sickness

I come before you prayerfully to testify once again of the goodness of our God.

Meditation Scriptures
Psalm 107:18-22 NIV

"They loathed all food and drew near the gates of death then they cried to the Lord in their trouble, and he saved them from their distress. He sent forth His word and healed them. He rescued them from the grave. Let them give thanks to the Lord for His unfailing love and His wonderful deeds for mankind. Let them sacrifice thank offerings and tell of His works with songs of joy."

Psalm 91:14-16 NIV

"Because he loves me says the Lord, I will rescue him. I will protect him for he acknowledges My name. He will call on me and I will answer him. I will be with him in trouble. I will deliver him and honor him, with long life will I satisfy him and show him my salvation."

Testimony:

Certain events will change your life forever. Barrenness is one of them. I was diagnosed with secondary infertility with no apparent reason. My husband and I tried to conceive for 5 years. The stress and heartache were wearing on the marriage, but we persevered, only with the help of God. In that fifth year God blessed us with twin babies. We were so excited for what God had done. The pregnancy and delivery were uneventful, but immediately after birth one of the them needed surgery. They rushed her to another hospital, with my husband in tow. She recovered, came home 14 days later from the NICU and we thought all our troubles were over. Fast forward, 17 days ahead and I find myself standing at the head of my daughter's hospital bed, in the pediatric intensive care unit. The doctor is informing me that she's not going to live through the night. She is 31 days old. She was diagnosed with pneumonia, croup, and influenza, while still recovering from surgery. No child survives all three respiratory complications at once! The nursing staff called for the chaplain to come to the bedside of my precious child. At this moment in my life, I had worked in the hospital for several years and from my experience it's never good when they call for the chaplain. This could indicate that death is inevitable. The chaplain was not able to bring me comfort, I think he had more anxiety than I did at that moment. There I was all alone, in the middle of the night, with a team of healthcare workers and a chaplain speaking and expecting the death of my newborn. Immediately, I called my husband. I told him to get to the hospital as soon as he could, because they're telling me our daughter...the one that we prayed for over five years, was not going to make it. The medical professionals were stating that she would die that night. I cried out and questioned God. Why would You do this to us? Why would You take her away when you made us wait so long for her? Why persevere God, if this is Your will? My husband came to the hospital making sure he brought worship music to change the atmosphere. He kicked everyone out of the room. He told me God did not bring her here to take her away from us. We need to plead and cry out to God, and He will save her. He said, what happened to your faith? Sometimes people in our environment can cause us to forget who we are and the authority we have. We both laid our hands on our child. She looked up at us unable to speak, helpless and suffering to breathe. We cried out to God and ask Him to heal her. We declared that we understood His power. We remembered His promises and we knew that he bought her to this earth for a purpose. We prayed, please God, don't take her away from us. We then began to speak to our baby, telling her to fight. We told her that she was a warrior. We declared, she's a child of God. We told her she was chosen to come to this earth for a purpose and she had to fight like she never fought before. Immediately her fever broke, she began to breathe better, her oxygen saturation improved, and over the course of the next day she was able to be discontinued from all breathing apparatus. The doctors could not explain. They kept stating, there's just no way. No child survives that! She has no immunity. She's only 31 days old! However, we know who the Doctor of all doctors is. JESUS and the power of His blood was her immunity. We told the doctors that we have Jesus' personal number. It's called PRAYER, combined with FAITH, to command the atmosphere. God gave us power in our mouth. **Matthew 18:19-20 NIV** *"Again truly I tell you that if two of you on earth agree about anything they ask for it will be done for them by my Father in heaven for where two or three gather in My name there am I with them."*

That wasn't the end of the journey. For the first two years of her life my child had a hospital stay each month for respiratory illness. As part of my praise report, I am delighted to tell you she has grown into a sweet, bright, vibrant, and healthy child. It wasn't easy, but looking back, it was a light affliction that we had to persevere through.

Prayer

God, I come before You with a humble and thankful heart. I know that I will be afflicted in this lifetime. I also know that You are a healer. You have proven it to me multiple times, not only in Your word, but in my lifetime. Lord, You are able to do exceedingly and abundantly above anything that I can ever imagine. I just need to activate the faith that lives within me. Help me to stand on Your word each day. For the heavens and the earth will pass away before Your word does. I ask that You supernaturally touch my body right now. Physically, mentally and emotionally, in the name of Jesus. I bind up sickness at its root and I command it back to the pit of hell, from where it came. I release the healing power of Jesus Christ over my life. Lord, You said by Your stripes I am healed, and I believe You today...if You can raise Lazarus from the dead, You can heal my body. You are the creator of the heavens and the earth. What could You not do? I thank You for all that You have done and for the miracles You will perform In Jesus Name Amen.

Healing Scriptures to Declare and Pray through Affliction

Isaiah 53:5 NIV
*"But he was pierced for our transgressions,
he was crushed for our iniquities; the punishment that
brought us peace was on Him, and by His wounds we are
healed."*

Isaiah 54:10 NIV
*"Though the mountains be shaken and the hills be removed, yet
My unfailing love for you will not be shaken, nor My covenant of
peace be removed, says the Lord, who has compassion on you."*

Jeremiah 17 :14 NIV
*"Heal me, Lord, and I will be healed; save me and I will be
saved, for you are the one I praise."*

Psalm 107:19-21 NIV
*"Then they cried to the LORD in their trouble, and he saved
them from their distress. 20 He sent out His word and healed
them; He rescued them from the
grave. 21 Let them give thanks to the Lord for His unfailing love
and His wonderful deeds for mankind."*

Jeremiah 33:6 NIV
*"Nevertheless, I will bring health and healing to it, I will heal my
people and will let them enjoy abundance of peace and security."*

1 Peter 2:24 NIV
*"He Himself bore our sins in His body on the cross, so that we
might die to sin and live for righteousness. By His wounds you
have been healed."*

Psalm 41:3 NIV
*"The Lord sustains them on their sickbed; and restores them
from their bed of illness."*

Psalm 147:3 NIV
"He heals the brokenhearted and binds up their wounds."

Proverbs 17:22 NIV
"A cheerful heart is good medicine, but a crushed spirit dries up the bones."

James 5:15 NIV
"And the prayer offered in faith will make the sick person well; the Lord will raise them up if they have sinned, they will be forgiven, therefore, confess your sins to each other and pray for each other, so that you may be healed, the prayer of a righteous person is powerful and effective."

3 John 1:2 NIV
"Dear friend I pray that you may enjoy good health and that all may go well with you even as your soul is getting along well."

Perseverance Through Loss

I pray that you are blessed, persevering through every circumstance in your life and believing God will bring comfort to you, if you are experiencing loss in any area of your life. Maybe it is the death of a loved one, the loss of a friendship, or the feeling that you are being stripped of everything in this season of your life.

Meditation Scriptures

Psalm 73:26 NIV

"My flesh and my heart may fail but God is the strength of my heart and my portion forever."

Psalm 147:3 NIV

"He heals the brokenhearted and binds up their wounds; He determines the number of stars and calls them each by name; great is our Lord and mighty in power; His understanding has no limit."

Revelation 21:4 NIV

"He will wipe every tear from their eyes, there will be no more death, or mourning, or crying, or pain; for the old order of things have passed away."

Testimony

Many of us may have experienced loss in all three areas mentioned above at some point in our lives. I can attest to that. However, the Holy Spirit has led me to focus on the loss of a loved one in this testimony. Nothing can prepare you for the loss of someone who holds a dear place in your heart. Twelve years ago, I unexpectedly lost my cousin Corey. Corey was more than a cousin; he was my brother. We grew up together and He was and is still deeply loved. I will never forget where I was when I received the news. I was in the hospital with my one-year-old, who was admitted for another bout of pneumonia. We were excited because she had recovered, and she was being discharged. My aunt called me and gave me the news over the phone, that he died from an asthma attack in his home. An asthma exacerbation! There was no way a healthy twenty something-year-old man dies from an asthma attack. I simply told her she was being untruthful and that I could not accept this news. I said I would call her later, because she must have gotten the message mixed up. Our minds have a funny way of helping us to protect ourselves. The first stage of grief is denial. When I was finally able to accept it...my immediate reaction was anger towards God. I shouted out to God, why would you take him? Of all the people on this earth who were so bad; why would you take one of the kindest, gentlest, illuminating people on the face of the earth? Why not someone who deserved to die? He was about to get married; he was going to be a new father. His first baby was being hand made in her mother's womb. What type of God would do such a thing? I told God that I was angry with Him and there was no way that I could come to terms with what He allowed to happen. I remained in that state for a few months. I was so angry with God that I could not pray. How could I pray to God when He hurt me so deeply. Oh, but the Holy Spirit has a way of comforting you. God has a way of allowing you to know, it is only by His grace and love that you can be healed. One morning, I was driving home from work after completing a night shift. I was talking in my car to Corey. Whenever I missed him, I talked to him as if he were next to me. I told Corey, if you are in heaven (because my faith was shaky, I didn't know what to believe), I need you to talk to God for me, because I can't pray. I knew that praying was the only way that I could hear from God and allow the Holy Spirit to comfort me. I told Corey, I have tried, but I'm too heartbroken. I do not know what to say. At that very moment, my phone rang. My sister Ashley told me that she had a dream, and she had to call me. She said Corey came to her in her dream and he had a message for me. Corey told her, God said He hears my every cry. He hears me even when I feel I'm not able to pray, because He knows my heart. He has not left me, but he's been here with me all the time. Immediately, as the tears rolled down my face, I repented. How could I think that a God who loves me would ever leave me. Wasn't I the one who was always proclaiming, He promised never to leave or forsake me. He promised to be my healing balm. I will never understand why Corey died or why God allows certain things to happen to us, but I know that God is the architect of my life. He has the blueprints! His ways are not like my ways. His plans are not like my plans. I am to trust Him through the process while accepting what transpired. I must persevere through the process. I must continue to push through. That's not to say it doesn't hurt my soul; for I have been wounded, but God will sustain me. Amen

Prayer

God, I come before you humbly with a prayerful heart. Thank you for always being my comforter, no matter the circumstance. You told me that there was a time and a season for everything under the sun. I pray for myself and anyone who may be mourning the death of someone they love. I pray for the losses in all areas of my life too. Lord, embrace me with your love. Shelter me. Heal me. Give me the endurance that I need to withstand this trial. Remind me that You are here God. You are always with me. You never left me. Thank you for answering my prayer, I count it as already done in Jesus' name Amen.

Prayer THREE

God thank You for this day and for the many blessings that you have bestowed upon me. Thank you for my trials and tribulations as I continue to walk through them, for I know that You are walking with me. Thank you for the little that I have, whether it is a little bit of hope, a little bit of finances/money, a little bit of love, or a little bit of peace. Whatever little I have, I know that You are able to make it more than enough. You are able to make it plenty. Jesus, You had two little fish and five loaves of bread, and you fed the multitude. You fed five thousand people, with food that was only enough to feed a few. Therefore, I come before You asking you to make my little more, in your timing. I know that sometimes things that begin small can become big. It requires a small seed to be planted to become a tree. I know that faith the size of a mustard seed is the amount needed to move mountains out of my life. I know who You are. The God of the universe, who can take my little and make it much. Thank You for always providing for me; letting me know that Your grace is more than sufficient for me; for reminding me that everything on earth belongs to You and the fullness thereof. In my season of lack, thank You for having and providing everything that I need. I will take my little bit of trust and ask that you expand it, so that it can multiply into Faith. I declare God, that you only want to prosper me, in Jesus' name Amen.

The Inheritance for Perseverance... "Take Up Your Cross"!

Grace and peace. My prayer for you is that God would remind
you that there is a reward for perseverance. The reward for taking
up your cross and bearing it, will be the inheritance of
abundance. God's glory will be established here on the earth by
the evidence shown in your life.

Meditation Scriptures
1 Corinthians 10: 31 NIV *"so whether you eat or drink or
whatever you do, do it all for the glory of God."*
Galatians 6:9 NIV *"Let us not become weary in doing good, for
at the proper time we will reap a harvest, if we do not give up."*

Colossians 3:23 NIV *"Whatever you do, work at it with all your
heart, as working for the Lord and not for men, since you know
that you will receive an inheritance from the Lord, as a reward it
is the Lord Christ you are serving."*

1 Corinthians 2:9-10 tells us that *"no eyes have seen, no ear has
heard, no mind has conceived what God has prepared for those
who love him."* The only way to get a glimpse into what He has
stored up for you is for God to reveal it to you by His Spirit...the
Holy Spirit. The Spirit of the Lord wants you to persevere
through the crushing and refining process. As a result, you will

bear fruit that will change lives for the kingdom of God. God will bless you abundantly. It will be more than you can ask for or even imagine. While it is OK to seek godly counsel from the elders or our sisters and brothers in Christ about our circumstances/condition or making difficult decisions; we must go to the Source first. We must go to the architect of our lives, Jesus. He has the blueprints! Stop murmuring and complaining. Stop consulting the project managers in your life and go to the architect. After all, you are his design and He knows the end result. He knows exactly what He is building and how it will be established. Have faith...trust in the process and the reward will be worth it. The greatest reward will be, you walking in your purpose perfectly, lacking nothing, steadfast, grounded and planted in God. Amen.

Prayer

God, I come before You with a thankful heart. I am so grateful that You have given me Your word to stand on and that You have designed me in your image and in your likeness. You have designed me to do important things for Your kingdom. Help me to propel into my purpose. Help me to persevere through every storm in my life, so that I may come out of the refining process as pure as gold. Help me not to murmur and to complain while I endure the trials and tribulations of life. Remind me that You are always right there with me. I declare that You are carrying me through, sheltering me under your wing, and being my rear guard. I know that there is a bountiful inheritance waiting for me, on the other side of my current circumstance. Thank You for answering prayers and the miracles that You will perform in my life. In Jesus Name Amen

<u>Rebranding the Remnant: Speak Life</u>

A Remnant is defined by Webster's dictionary as a small remaining quantity of something. God has called us to speak life over every situation and every remnant, no matter how big or small! My prayer for you today is that you would gather the remnant, open your mouth, and speak to it.

Proverbs 18:21 tells us, *"Death and life are in the power of the tongue and those who love it will eat its fruit."* Jesus is the bread of life and all who partake of Him have the power of life in their words, because He lives on the inside of us. Jesus raised from the dead and so can every promise, dream, or ambition that we have laid to rest. Those things that we feel hopeless about requires that we speak over them. We must have faith and open our mouths to unleash the power of God in our lives, to birth the promises He has in store for us.

Meditation Scriptures
Romans 4:17 NKJV

"As it is written, I have made you a father of many nations in the presence of Him whom he believed - God gives life to the dead and calls those things which do not exist as though they did."

Abraham became what was spoken over him, because his faith met God's word and produced fruit! So shall we! No matter how

the situation may appear, WHAT GOD HAS PROMISED HE IS
ABLE TO PERFORM.

Jesus spoke over the little bread and fish He had and was able to
feed five thousand. How many people will you feed with your
God given gifts and talents?

John 6:12 NIV states *"so when they were filled, He said to His
disciples Gather up the fragments that remain, so that nothing is
lost."*

Jesus fed the five thousand who were hungry and still had
leftovers. Just as Jesus instructed His disciples not to let the
remnant go to waste, He instructs us to gather the fragments of
what's left of our dreams, our aspirations, our businesses, our
family relationships, our mental health, our marriages, our hopes;
so that none is loss. He wants to take what's left and rebrand it!
He wants to give us a new name! He wants to rebrand us,
because He has more to give us and more for us to do, so that His
kingdom can be established here on earth, as it is in heaven.
(Matthew 6:9-10)

Prayer:
*God, I come before You to thank You for the remnant. I
recognize that despite going through many trials and tribulations
I still have a little that remains. Therefore, I activate my faith*

and speak over that little so that it can grow and become something new. Something big, that looks like Your promises being fulfilled in my life. Holy Spirit, I give You permission to do as You will, so that Your kingdom can be established on this earth as it is in heaven. I hear You calling me to come back to my rightful place; to be in the right posture. Use me as Your vessel, as Your hands and feet here on the earth. Thank You for even considering me! I bless You, because I know that if I should ask anything in Your name and it is according to Your will it shall be done! Thank You for being such a good Father to me. Hallowed be thy name! I give You all the glory and honor forever and ever Amen.

Waiting

As we continue to embark on this journey, my prayer for you is that you begin to recognize that God remembers you and He knows the substance of your being. Many times, we must go through seasons of waiting; waiting for our dreams to transpire, waiting for deliverance from the strongholds we have been struggling with, waiting for financial breakthrough, waiting for healing, waiting for a sign from God to move or launch into our next. Sometimes, when we are waiting the enemy tricks us into believing that because we have been waiting for so long, God has forgotten about us. I have been given an assignment to let you know that God remembers you and he knows your name! For it is written, in **Psalm 139: 15 -16 NIV** *"my frame was not hidden from You, when I was made in the secret place, when I was woven together in the depths of the earth, your eyes saw my unformed body, all the days ordained for me, were written in your book, before one of them came to be."*

This means God knew what all of your days would entail, before we even lived them! He knows the substance of what you are made of, because he wove it together, before you were even formed. He knows everything that you are going to face, every season you are going to endure, every emotion you are going to feel, every decision you have ever made, and He has equipped you for it! Because when He formed you, He placed in you everything that you would need to live the life that He ordained for you. Your characteristics as well as your gifts are not by chance, but God, who remembers you, placed them on the inside of you, as tools to utilize while you are waiting.

Therefore, while you are waiting begin to pray, praise and worship! Be comforted knowing that it is written in **Jeremiah 29:11** *"God knows the plans He has for you, plans to prosper you and not to harm you, plans to give you hope and a future."* Know that when you call upon Him and come and pray to Him,

He will listen to you. You are not abandoned; God is with you and will never leave you.

We make this DECLARATION today that God walks with us daily, never leaving, nor forsaking us, He is a constant in our life, even when others are not for, it is written in **Deuteronomy 31:6** *"Be strong, and of good courage, do not fear do not be afraid of them for the Lord, your God, He is the one who goes with you. He will not leave you or forsake you."*

Prayer

Spirit of the living God I come before You with thanksgiving, knowing that You have not forgotten me. You have not abandoned me. You remember me and You know my name. I ask You to take total control of my mind and heart today. When the enemy of my very soul tries to trick me; when he whispers to me that I am irrelevant and that You will not answer me, I pray that the Holy Spirit on the inside of me comes alive, to combat the lies with your truth. Remind me that it is written that I am precious in your sight. I come against the spirit of desperation, depression and discouragement. Lord, send those spirits back to the pit of hell. It is written that you did not give me a spirit of fear, but of power, love, and self-discipline. You gave me a sound mind. The joy of the Lord will be my strength today! Let Your Kingdom come, Your will be done in my life as it is in heaven! I bless You and thank You In Jesus Name Amen.

Prayer FOUR

*God, thank You for all that You are doing in my life and for
sending your Son Jesus Christ, to die on the cross for my sins.
Thank You for making a way back to you and for sending Him to
break every chain and curse, which has been spoken over my life
for generations to come. When I am in covenant with You, every
curse is broken. Please help me to uphold and keep my end of
the bargain. You are always faithful; never give up on me; never
leave me nor forsake me. You are always here. It is me who
turned away from you. Sometimes I think that I know better,
when I try to take the reins of my life. Break every single chain,
break every curse that has been spoken over me and my
descendants. Break it Jesus! Break every yoke and help me to
take your yoke which is easy and light. God, as You break the
chains, bind up the enemy with them, in the name of Jesus. I ask
you to bind sickness, hopelessness, depression and anxiety, in
exchange, please loose the peace of God which surpasses all
understanding, joy and happiness. It can only come from You.
God, we give You permission to take total control, take the reins.
I surrender to You, knowing I am being broken only to be put
back together, better for purpose. I look to the hills where my
help comes from. It will only come from You. It is not going to be
by my power or might, but it's going to be by Your Spirit. Help
me to remember not to be anxious for anything, but in everything*

by prayer and supplication, with Thanksgiving to make my request made known to You and the God of peace will give me peace, which will guard my heart and my mind in Christ Jesus. God send your word to enter the battlefield of my mind. Speak over my life, so that the word You sent will match up with the word that lives within me. That word will activate the Holy Spirit that lives on the inside of me and bring forth the fruit You desire from me. God, I trust you, no matter what the circumstances look like, I love you and I worship you today, in Jesus' name Amen.

<u>Chosen, Anointed and Appointed</u>

I pray that this passage reminds you of who you are and of the many gifts and talents that the Father has bestowed upon & within you.

Meditation Scriptures:

John15:16 NIV, *"you did not choose me, but I chose you and appointed you, so that you might go bear fruit that will last and so whatever you ask in My name the Father will give you."*

Mark 4:21 NIV *"He said to them, do you bring in a lamp to put it under a bowl or a bed? Instead, don't you put it on a stand? For whatever is hidden is meant to be disclosed and whatever is concealed is meant to be brought out into the open."*

Before you were placed in your mother's womb, you were and still are chosen, appointed and anointed! You may be in a season of your life where you feel like you are not walking in your God given purpose. You may even question if the anointing, He has placed deep down on the inside of you, has ceased to exist. I am here to tell you that your feelings have lied to you. What God has created will live until its purpose is fulfilled. The gifts, talents and anointing are not dead. **John 15:16 NIV** reads:

"You did not choose Me I chose you and appointed you that you should go and bear fruit and that your fruit should remain that whatever you ask the Father in My name He may give you." You are chosen to bear fruit that will remain! God selected you before the foundation of the earth was laid, for a specific assignment. Therefore, it is time to come out of your dormant state and recognize who you are.

Mark 4:21 NIV

"Also, He said to them, is a lamp brought to be put under a basket or under a bed? Is it not to set up on a lampstand?"
Before humans knew how to channel currents so that we could utilize electricity, oil filled lamps were used to illuminate dark spaces. Each one of us has a specific anointing to accomplish different assignments, which have been ordained by God. Metaphorically speaking, we have all been filled with oil so that we can illuminate the dark places too. The oil in your lamp represents the anointing that is within you. Until you allow the oil to burn, the light cannot be reproduced. The light that the world so desperately needs. The light which can only come from you.

If you are feeling hopeless or feel as if the gifts you witnessed in a previous season of your life are dead, re-evaluate the situation and call out to your Heavenly Father. He can change the course and bring life to that dead state of mind, just as He added life to Hezekiah after he called out to the Lord. **(II Kings 20:1-7NIV).** I declare that Your anointing is still there! Your gifts are still your current course! You are still chosen! You have just covered your light with the basket of life's hardships. It is time to remember who God said you are, set your lamp on the lampstand…come out of hiding and let your light shine!

Prayer

God, thank You for choosing, anointing and appointing me for such a time as this. You knew me before You placed me in my mother's womb and gave me an assignment to accomplish here on earth. Help me to remember who You say I am, so that I may bear fruit that remains. Lord combat the spirit of discouragement and every lie that I have believed about who I am. God, take my thoughts captive and bring them into alignment with your thoughts about me and who You have called me to be. Thank You for choosing me and for allowing me to always have victory over the enemy of my soul. In Jesus Name, Amen.

Refining and Expansion

My prayer for you today is that you trust in God, as He refines and expands you. God knows your capacity to expand and wants to enlarge your territory.

Many times when we cry out to God for more blessings, anointing, advancement or to be more like Him, we fail to realize, in order to receive more the cost is expansion. Simply put, God has to make room in order for us to receive more. Stretching and expanding can be uncomfortable and sometimes downright painful. However, making room is part of the refining process, it's uncomfortable, but it's necessary. The pain is temporary. We must remember, we asked God for it, and He always Listens! As it is written in, **I Chronicle 4:9-10 NIV** *"Jabez was more honorable than his brothers. his mother named him Jabez, saying I gave birth to him in pain. Jabez cried out to the God of Israel, "Oh, that You would bless me and enlarge my territory! Let Your hand be with me and keep me from harm so that I will be free from pain." And God granted his request."*

Sometimes we believe that we lack the capacity for one more thing! One more responsibility, one more encounter with that person, one more illness, one more engagement on our calendar etc. etc. When we go through the issues of life, we forget that our

Creator who remembers us, who called us by name, has given us the anointing and the capacity to do all that he has set before us. Hence, when you are feeling overwhelmed, you must tap into the anointing that dwells on the inside of you. Recognize that it's not going to be by your power, or your might, but it's going to be by His Spirit that you will be able to grow gracefully, expand, and receive all that God has for you. It is written in **Zechariah 4:6 NIV** *"So He said to me, "This is the word of the Lord to Zerubbabel: 'Not by might nor by power, but by my Spirit,' says the Lord Almighty."* It is written in **I John 2:20,27 NIV** (20) *"But you have an anointing from the Holy One, and all of you know the truth. (27) As for you, the anointing you received from Him remains in you, and you do not need anyone to teach you. But as His anointing teaches you about all things and as that anointing is real, not counterfeit-just as it has taught you, remain in Him."*

The key to not shredding under the pressure of being stretched is to abide in Him. As long as you are in alignment with His word and rest in His presence while abiding, you will not be shaken. God will have compassion on you. He promises to give you peace no matter what happens on the earth during your lifetime, because He loves you. It is written in **Isaiah 54:10 NIV** *"Though the mountains be shaken, and the hills be removed yet My unfailing love for you will not be shaken, nor My covenant of*

peace be removed. says the Lord, who has compassion on you."
Therefore, stop relying on your own strength rely on His and do
as He instructed you, in order to receive what He has for you. As
it is written in **Isaiah 54:2-5 NIV** *"Enlarge the place of your tent
stretch your tent curtains wide, do not hold back; lengthen your
cords, strengthen your stakes. For you will spread out to the
right and to the left, your descendants will dispossess nations
and settle in their desolate cities. Do not be afraid; you will not
be put to shame, do not fear disgrace; you will not be humiliated.
You will forget the shame of your youth and remember no more
the reproach of your widowhood. For your Maker is your
husband the Lord Almighty is His name the Holy One of Israel is
Isaiah your Redeemer; he is called the God of all the earth."*

God loves you and He wants His glory to be shown in the earth
so others can be drawn to Him. God gives insight, for it is written
in **Isaiah 48:10-11 NIV** *"See, I have refined you, though not as
silver; I have tested you in the furnace of affliction. For my own
sake, for my own sake, I do this. How can I let myself be
defamed? I will not yield my glory to another."* Therefore,
endure this refining season. You have the capacity to do so. It is
written in **Psalm 29:11 NIV** *"The Lord gives strength to His
people; the Lord blesses His people with peace."*

Declaration

I decree and declare that God will carry me through every obstacle or challenging situation in my life. When I am weak, He is strong. He will restore my soul, in Jesus' name, as it is written in **Isaiah 12:2** *"surely God is my salvation. I will trust, and not be afraid the Lord the Lord himself is my strength and my defense he has become my salvation,"* and in **Zechariah 4:6** *"not by might, nor by power, but by My Spirit says the Lord Almighty."*

Prayer

God I surrender! I know now that You have given me the capacity to face every obstacle that comes my way. I thank You for the anointing that lives on the inside of me. The anointing that destroys the yoke of the enemy. Allow the Holy Spirit to comfort me as I endure the growing pains. You have remarkable things in store for me! So, as I enter this refining process, help me to abide in You and let Your peace that passes all understanding guard my heart and mind in Christ Jesus. Thank You for trusting me with the anointing and the assignment. Continue to walk with me daily. I praise You for what You are doing in the earth and in me. Lord, let Your kingdom come and Your will be done in my life as it is in heaven, in Jesus' name amen.

Combating the Lies with the Truth

My prayer for you today is that you would combat every lie of the enemy with the truth of God's word. It is written in **Ephesians 6:12 NIV** *"For our struggle is not against flesh and blood, but against the rulers, against the authorities, against the powers of this dark world and against the spiritual forces of evil in the heavenly realms."*

When Jesus went into the wilderness, the enemy of his soul attempted to divert Him from His purpose by telling Him lies. The enemy tried to tempt Jesus by making false promises. It is written in **Luke 4:1-13 NIV** *"Jesus, full of the Holy Spirit, left the Jordan and was led by the Spirit into the wilderness, where for forty days He was tempted by the devil. He ate nothing during those days, and at the end of them he was hungry. The devil said to Him, "If you are the Son of God, tell this stone to become bread." Jesus answered, "It is written: 'Man shall not live on bread alone.' The devil led Him up to a high place and showed Him in an instant all the kingdoms of the world. And he said to Him, "I will give You all their authority and splendor; it has been given to me, and I can give it to anyone I want to. " If You worship me, it will all be Yours. "Jesus answered, "It is written: 'Worship the Lord your God and serve him only. The devil led Him to Jerusalem and had Him stand on the highest point of the temple. "If you are the Son of God," he said, "throw yourself* *down from here. For it is written:" 'He will command his angels concerning You to guard you carefully; they will lift You up in their hands, so that You will not strike your foot against a stone. Jesus answered, "<u>It is said</u>: 'Do not put the Lord your God to the test.'? When the devil had finished all this tempting, he left him until an opportune time."* If the enemy did it to Jesus, he will do it to you! Notice, the enemy knows the word of God too, but he twists and perverts it, to not only trick us, but to prevent us from walking in purpose.

Jesus did not fight the enemy from a place of emotions or feelings. He didn't say well "I know my truth "and fight based on His emotions and irritation. He combated the enemy with The Truth of God's word. His response was <u>IT IS WRITTEN</u>. Jesus knew the truth of God 's word and trusted in it. We too, as disciples and followers of Christ, must put total trust in what God has said about us, our situations, trials, tribulations and the various seasons of our lives. We too must combat the lies of the enemy with the truth of God's word.

The word of God is your weapon. It is written in **Ephesians 6:13-17 NIV** *"Therefore put on the full armor of God, so that when the day of evil comes, you may be able to stand your ground, and after you have done everything, to stand. Stand firm then, with the belt of truth buckled around your waist, with the* *breastplate of righteousness in place, and with your feet fitted with the readiness that comes from the gospel of peace. In addition to all this, take up the shield of faith, with which you can extinguish all the flaming arrows of the evil one. Take the helmet of salvation and the sword of the Spirit, which is the word of God."*

The only way you will learn how to use the word is to know it for yourself. How can you fight against the enemy of your soul if you do not know how to use your weapons? How do you know what is truth, when you don't know the words written about who you are and what God has promised you in this lifetime? It is written in **Joshua 1:8 NIV** *"Keep this Book of the Law always on your lips; meditate on it day and night, so that you may be careful to do everything written in it. Then you will be prosperous and successful."* In **Psalm 119:10 NIV,** *"I seek You with all my heart, do not let me stray from Your commands. I have hidden Your word in my heart that I might not sin against You."*

How do you know that the voices you hear are of God, yourself, or the enemy of your soul? You must sharpen your weapons! These are commands not just suggestions! When the general in the army gives his soldiers commands, they follow them, because they trust that his experience and expertise will not fail them. You must test the spirit behind words, actions and encounters by the Holy Spirit that dwells on the inside of you. God will never contradict His word. His word and His promises never fail and will never fade away. It is written in **I John 4:1 NIV** *"Dear friends, do not believe every spirit, but test the spirits to see whether they are from God, because many false prophets have gone out into the world."* In **Luke 1:37 NIV** *"For no word from God will ever fail."* It is written in **Luke 21:33** *"Heaven and earth will pass away, but my words will never pass away."* How can you put such trust in man and not in the Creator who remembers you, knows the substance of your being, the tools you have been equipped with and your capacity to accomplish the tasks He has put before you? It is written in **Psalm 146:3-6 NIV** *"Do not put your trust in princes, in human beings, who cannot save. When their spirit departs, they return to the ground; on that very day their plans come to nothing. Blessed are those whose help is the God of Jacob, whose hope is in the LORD their God. He is the Maker of heaven and earth, the sea, and everything in them—He remains faithful forever."*

God wrote your manuscript He knows how things are going to play out…trust Him.

Declaration

I decree and declare that no evil shall befall me or my family no plan, trap, or snare will prosper. I will combat the lies of the enemy with the truth That is God's word. I will trust God and hide His word in my heart that I might not sin against Him. In Jesus Name.

Prayer

God thank You for giving Me Your word that I may use as a weapon to fight against the enemy of my soul. Help me to study Your word, so that I can show myself approved. When the enemy attempts to come against me with his lies I will fight back with Your word. No longer will I fight based on my emotions, feelings, or my own truths. I will fight with THE TRUTH that comes from scripture. Take total control over my heart and mind today. Hearken my ears to hear Your voice. Give me the desire to spend more time in prayer and meditation on the scriptures, so that when You speak, I don't miss it. Continue to establish your will in my life, as it is in heaven, in Jesus' name Amen.

Prayer FIVE

God, I come before you as humbly as I know how, to Your throne of grace. Thank You for giving me this opportunity to speak with You once again. I do not take it lightly when You commune with me. Thank You for all Your marvelous works that you perform each day on the earth. The very fact that I am able to wake up in the morning and have breath in my lungs is a miracle. As long as I have breath, I have purpose. Thank You for the plans that You have ordained for my life. Even in the midst of chaos You bring me comfort. You know all things, even when I do not. Help me to lean not on my own understanding, but to acknowledge You in all my ways that so You will make my path straight. Thank You for breaking generational curses and for establishing my gifts on the earth. Before the foundation of the earth, You knew what I was coming to this earth to do. Help me not to abort the mission which You sent me to earth to accomplish. I look to You, so that I am in alignment with what You're trying to do in my life. Lord, help me to combat against the spirit of darkness and any principality that is unlike you. Cleanse my atmosphere in the mighty name of Jesus, so that Your Spirit may be established here. I will not fear, but I will walk in my divine power. My mouth has the power of life and death. I speak life right now into every dead situation. In this home I give you authority in the name of Jesus, to take hold of anything unlike You. I come against the spirit of witchcraft, right now, in the name of Jesus and loose the Holy Spirit which has divine power and dominion over all things. Anything that's trying to prevent me from locking into my destiny, arrest it Holy Spirit. Allow the Holy Spirit to dwell where I am. Let Your peace rest upon me. Saturate me from the crown of my head to the sole of my feet by Your blood. Nothing can come against the blood of Jesus. Let me walk in boldness for I count it as done knowing that anything I ask for in prayer shall be done if it's according to Your will. Let Your Kingdom come, and Your will be done in my life, as it is in heaven, in Jesus' name, Amen.

Cultivation

My prayer for you today is that you allow God to cultivate your gifts. By doing so you will discover who you really are and build your life on the foundation that is Him. He wants you to use that foundation to build the Kingdom of God. Rid yourselves of the destruction that toxic comparison brings. God is refining you and knows the capacity that you must expand as He enlarges your territory. God wants you to combat the lies of the enemy with THE TRUTH of His word ALL FOR HIS GLORY!

As you approach the start of each day make room for prayer and devotion each morning, to set the tone of your day. Put God first, by outwardly taking action to give Him all the praise and glory

He deserves. Go before Him with a thankful heart, no matter what your current circumstances or conditions appear to be. When you begin to praise God, the atmosphere has no choice but to shift. God loves and He hears you. For it is written in **Psalm 136:1-4 NIV** *"Give thanks to the LORD, for He is good. His love endures forever. Give thanks to the God of gods. His love endures forever. Give thanks to the Lord of lords: His love endures forever. to Him who alone does great wonders, His love endures forever."* It is also written in **Revelation 4:11 NIV** *"You are worthy, our Lord and God, to receive glory and honor and power, for You created all things, and by Your will they were created and have their being."*

All glory belongs to God the Creator of all things and when we allow our position in life, careers, family, circumstances, obstacles, people or things to become our main focus, those things become idols. They may not be physical statues of deities like the Israelites made, but when we place all of our attention, effort and focus there, and we neglect our relationship with God, we are outwardly saying those things are more important. By doing this we are taking advantage of God's love and grace for us. It is written in **Romans 1:21-23 NIV** *"For although they knew God, they neither glorified Him as God nor gave thanks to Him, but their thinking became futile, and their foolish hearts were darkened. 22 Although they claimed to be wise, they* *became fools 23 and exchanged the glory of the immortal God for images made to look like a mortal human being and birds and animals and reptiles."* It is also written in **Jonah 2:8-9 NIV** *"Those who cling to worthless idols turn away from God's love for them. But I, with shouts of grateful praise, will sacrifice to You. What I have vowed I will make good. I will say, 'Salvation comes from the LORD.' "*

I recognize it's sometimes hard and we lose focus, because we are all human. The time has come to shift your focus and come into alignment with who God needs you to be on the earth. The only way to discover this is by drawing close to Him and living your life to bring Him glory in everything you do. It is written in **I Corinthians 10:31 NIV** *"So whether you eat or drink or whatever you do, do it all for the glory of God."* In **II Corinthians 4:15-18 NIV** *"All this is for your benefit, so that the grace that is reaching more and more people may cause thanksgiving to overflow to the glory of God. 16 Therefore, we do not lose heart. Though outwardly we are wasting away, yet inwardly we are being renewed day by day. 17 For our light and momentary troubles are achieving for us an eternal glory that far outweighs them all. 18 So we fix our eyes, not on what is seen, but on what is unseen, since what is seen is temporary, but what is unseen is eternal."*

Never forget to recognize who God is, how His love abounds,

and how important it is to abide in Him. For it is written in **Psalm 108:4 NIV** *"For great is Your love, higher than the heavens; Your faithfulness reaches to the skies. 5 Be exalted, O God, above the heavens; let Your glory be over all the earth."*

Declaration

I decree and declare that the favor of God is over my life, His lovingkindness towards me, and for generations to come, is my portion as it is written in **Psalm 5:12**, *"surely Lord you bless the righteous you surround them with your favor, as with a shield."* I know as it is written in **Romans 8:28** *"all things will work together for my good, because I love Him and I am called according to His purpose."* I declare that God will get all the glory from my life in Jesus' name. Amen

Prayer

God, thank You for giving me breath today, for as long as I have breath, I have purpose. Thank You for giving me the opportunity to worship and praise You, and give You all the glory that You deserve. Words cannot encapsulate all that You have done for me and continue to do in my life. Help me to draw near to You, abide in You and allow You to complete the good work that You have activated in me. My life will demonstrate Your glory here on the earth. I give the Holy Spirit total permission for the establishment of your kingdom in my heart, mind and life, in Jesus' name, amen.

Humility-Stripped-Prepared for Exaltation

My prayer is that you would Allow the Holy Spirit to tear down the walls that you have built and make room in your heart for Jesus.

When Mary, the mother of Jesus, was giving birth to her Son, who was to be called Immanuel, there was no room for Him to rest His head. Can you imagine that the One who was promised, who was coming to deliver us was turned away by individuals, who didn't have insight into who He was, or what promise He held. Was there not one among them who had vision and foresight? His name literally means "God is with us and Yahweh saves" He is and was the answer to everything that we need.

Matthew 1:21-25 NKJV states *"And she will bring forth a Son and you shall call His name Jesus, for He will save His people from their sins, so all this was done that it might be fulfilled, which was spoken by the Lord through the prophet saying, behold a virgin shall be with child and bear a Son and they shall call his name Immanuel which is translated God with us. Then Joseph being aroused from sleep did as the angel of the Lord commanded him and took to him his wife and did not know her until she had brought forth her first born Son and he called His name Jesus"*. Are you making room? Room in your heart? Room in your mind? Room in every aspect of your being? There was no room to rest His head, but you can make room in every chamber of your heart! It is time to tear down the walls you have made and allow His Holy Spirit to rest in you so that you may have His peace and His joy abundantly.

Philippians 4:6-7 NKJV states *"Be anxious for nothing, but in everything, by prayer and supplication, with thanksgiving, let your requests be made known to God; and the peace of God, which surpasses all understanding, will guard your hearts and minds through Christ Jesus"* **Isaiah 26:3 NIV** reminds us *"He will keep in perfect peace those whose minds are steadfast, because they trust in Him"* and lastly **Romans 8:6 NIV** states *"the mind governed by the flesh is death, but the mind governed by the Spirit is life and peace."*

God wants you to have an abundant life…an abundance of peace, favor, joy, love and faith. In order to access abundance, you must humble yourself, trust Him and give Him complete control over every aspect of your being. God had a purpose when He came in the form of man…He humbled Himself, despite knowing who He was and the power that lived within Him. We must do the same. Move as a servant would move, not boastful, but with purpose. Allow Him to strip and prepare you. When you do you will be exalted for His glory. He will take you from the prison to the palace like Joseph; from the field to the throne like Ruth & Esther and most importantly, you will submit to the process like Jesus did. He went from heavenly places to human form, to the cross and exalted again at the right hand of the Father in the end.

Prayer

God, I give You permission to tear down every single wall. Every wall that may try to hinder me from what Your anointing wants to accomplish within me. I give you total access, authority and the dominion to make the walls of my heart fall like the walls of Jericho. Allow Your Holy Spirit to take possession of the land of my heart, mind and being. Let Your Spirit well up so much on the inside of me that there is room for nothing more. I intentionally make room for You in my heart, mind, and in my spirit. Let Your kingdom be established in my life, so that your glory may be revealed here on this earth through me. Allow me to be Your hands to accomplish the things that You have predestined, before the foundations of the earth. I bless You with the fruit of my lips. I now know that You are in fact Immanuel, God with us, because You are with me. Save me as Your name declares, in Jesus. Amen

Prayer SIX

God thank You for this day, this moment and for where You have brought me from. As I approach the days ahead, I want to specifically thank You for every obstacle You have helped me and my family to overcome. God, You have given me vision and though the vision tarries it will come to pass. Thank You, in advance, for the blessings that You're going to bestow upon me, for the grace that you have already provided for me, to make it through yet another year. I thank You God, for the many blessings that I have seen year after year, thank You for the trials and tribulations, which have helped me to become stronger in You. You have taught me to lean in and rely on Your strength and not my own. Cultivate the gifts that You have placed on the inside of me. Thank you for provision. God, You saw the season that was to come, and You helped me to prepare for it. As I approach my next, I enter it with gratitude. I may not see exactly what it is that you have planned, but I know that it will be good, based on the promises You have made to me. I trust You, knowing that more is to come, exceedingly and abundantly above anything that I can ever ask or imagine. I will not lack anything; my future looks promising. Thank You for the expansion of my belief, my gifts and the Holy Spirit. I thank You for the capacity to receive more, even when I feel that I am stretched to the limit. You know what I can handle and my full capacity. My latter is going to be greater than my former. I leave behind the past and take the bridge over into my future. When I get tired help me to remember that You will renew my strength and mount me up like an eagle, so that I can soar. Thank You for the word that You have placed in my heart. Allow the word to well up within me whenever I feel discouraged, knowing You have already given me the victory over the enemy. In every situation, let me not lean on my own understanding God, but instead acknowledge You in every way, so that You will make my path straight, in Jesus' name, Amen

<u>Illuminate the Dark Places</u>

Sometimes, God wants to illuminate the dark hidden places of our hearts and minds in order to heal us. Some wounds must be exposed to fresh air in order to heal. **James 5:16 NIV** tells us to *"therefore confess your sins to each other and pray for each other, so that you may be healed; the prayer of a righteous person is powerful and effective."*

Many of us have been consumed, attempting to keep our dark and hidden places from getting exposed. We fail to expose our traumas for fear of judgment. We don't want others to know that we are sick, wounded, or that an old wound has failed to heal properly. Sometimes we fail to recognize that our wounds and traumas have begun to seep out and affect those around us. The reality is, our trauma is spilling. It's leaving stains on everyone around us. Our family members, coworkers, friends, even our brothers and sisters in Christ.

James 5:13 NKJV states *"is anyone among you suffering? Let him pray. Is anyone cheerful? Let him sing psalms. Is anyone among you sick? Let him call for the elders of the church and let them pray over him, anointing him with oil in the name of the Lord. And the prayer of faith will save the sick and the Lord will raise him up. And if he has committed sins he will be forgiven."* Your life experiences have not been in vain, whether good, bad, or ugly. You are not supposed to harden your heart and cover up, but instead allow God to illuminate the dark places of your heart and mind. Only then can you get help and be healed. **1 Peter 5:5 NIV** tells us *"In the same way, you who are younger submit yourselves to your elders. All of you, clothe yourselves with humility toward one another, because God opposes the proud and shows favor to the humble."*

We cannot hide from God. God wants the church to be authentic not counterfeit. God is calling for us to bring our humbled, truthful, bare, trauma ridden selves to His throne of grace. **John 4:23-24 NKJV** *"But the hour is coming and now is, when the true worshippers will worship the Father in spirit and truth. For the Father is seeking such to worship Him. God is spirit and those who worship Him must worship in spirit and truth."*

Only when we go before Him and worship Him in Spirit and truth will He break the chains holding us back, so that our gifts and anointing can be unleashed.

Prayer

God thank You for giving me another day. Thank You for instructing me how to allow the illumination of the dark and hidden places of my heart and mind to expose the wounds, so that I may be healed. God, You told me to come out of darkness into the light. I know the power of your light. Therefore, I come before You to bare my heart and soul, worshipping in Spirit and

Truth. Break the chains and unleash the power and anointing, which comes from the Holy Spirit alone. Thank You for hearing my prayers. I count all that I have prayed for as done, if it is according to Your will. Continue to fill the rooms of my heart and mind. I will forever give Your name the honor and glory it deserves. In Jesus' name, Amen.

Freedom from Your Past...Propelling Towards Purpose

Many times, on our spiritual journey, God attempts to free us from positions, emotions, relationships, and thought processes that no longer serve a purpose in our lives. However, it's up to us to be obedient and grant permission to the Holy Spirit to do the work within us, to set us free and launch us into purpose. **Isaiah 43:18-19 NIV** states *"forget the former things do not dwell on the past, see I am doing a new thing now it springs up do you not perceive it? I am making a way in the wilderness and streams on the wasteland. "*

You may be thinking, I know that already. Do you know how long I've been saved and working on this sanctification process? I've been walking with Jesus for years. God is calling Zion to freedom from this mindset, to a posture of prayer and humility before Him. Only then can He perform new works within us and heal us from the trauma we have endured.

2 Chronicles 7:14 NIV states *"If my people, who are called by my name, would humble themselves and pray and seek my face and turn from their wicked ways, then I will hear from heaven and I will forgive their sin and heal their land."* Some may think, wicked? Gasp! Now you have gone too far. But **Proverbs 21:2-4 NIV** tells us that *"A person may think their own ways are right, but the Lord weighs the heart. To do what is right and just is*

more acceptable to the Lord than sacrifice. Haughty eyes and a proud heart - the unplowed field of the wicked- produce sin."
We must always remain humble and assume the role of a student when God is trying to teach us about who we are. He wants to deliver us from old habits and perspectives. Deliverance from the old way we view marriage, business, finances, sickness, depression and people. Out with the old and in with the new! Sometimes it's hard to understand why you must evolve. These old positions, emotions, relationships, or thought processes have served you in a way that protected you from perceived danger. Sometimes it's just comfort that makes it hard to change. Regardless, whether positive or negative, you must not fantasize about it, long for it, or stay in it. Many of your behaviors and mindsets were coping mechanisms, simply a crutch Keeping you in the old season of your life.

I Corinthians 13:11 NIV states *"when I was a child, I talked like a child I reasoned like a child, when I became a man, I put the ways of childhood behind me."*

What I have learned from the Holy Spirit through prayer is that when it is time to level up and fear sets in; I must recite the statement that God gave me. "It has served its purpose. Now say thank you to it, be free from it and move on; It was all a part of the building process meant to move me into my next."

True freedom comes from the Holy Spirit and learning to trust God throughout the process; no matter what the situation may look like. It's knowing that God is never going to fail you. He is faithful in His promises concerning you. **Psalm 34:4 NKJV** states *"I sought the Lord, and He heard me and delivered me from my fears."* **Jeremiah 29:12 NIV** states *"Then you will call on Me and come and pray to Me and I will listen to you."* God is always listening and always there to guide us through the various seasons of our lives. We just need to show up and meet Him with enough faith in an effort to walk in true freedom. How much is enough? Jesus states *"the size of a mustard seed."* **Luke 17:6 NIV**

Prayer

God, I come before You this day to say thank You for propelling me towards my purpose. Help me to let go of things that no longer serve me. Just as You moved Your presence from the tabernacle to the temple and into me, by giving me the Holy Spirit; I must continue to evolve into the creation that You have called me to be. Help me to walk in the freedom that only comes from trusting You, Your plan, and Your promises for my life. I know You will never fail me! I know you will never leave me nor forsake me, but that You are always here with me. You go before me. You're even behind me, watching my rear. Help me to realize God, that even though I may feel surrounded at times I am surrounded by You. I thank You for all that You are doing in my life and will forever give Your name the glory and honor that it deserves. In Jesus' name, Amen

Thankful Hearts During Crushing Moments

Grace and peace. My prayer for you is that you give thanks to God for every season of your life, knowing that He is the great architect of your being. He has purposed you for greatness, before you were even placed in your mother's womb. That's right, God specifically designed you for a purpose, before you were conceived. No one on the face of this earth has your exact same purpose. King David said it best when he stated in **Psalm 139:13 NIV** *"For you created my inmost being; you knit me together in my mother's womb. I praise you, because I am fearfully and wonderfully made; your works are wonderful; I know that full well. My frame was not hidden from You when I was made in the secret place, when I was woven together in the depths of the earth. Your eyes saw my unformed body; all the days ordained for me were written in Your book before one of them came to be."*

With this in mind, God has the blueprint for your life. He knows every challenge you will face, every disastrous moment that will come and above all the victory that will be had over every situation or circumstance. Therefore, you must stand firm and know that the crushing/pressing is a process that you should have a thankful heart towards. The crushing is what produces the oil, so that the anointing can flow from your life. **James 1:2 NIV** *"Consider it pure joy my brothers and sisters, whenever you face*

trials of many kinds, because you know that the testing of your
faith produces perseverance. Let perseverance finish its work so
that you may be mature and complete not lacking anything."
It's not easy to thank God for the trials and tribulations.
However, if you recognize what these moments produce, you
will align yourself with God's will and declare…Lord let your
will be done and your kingdom come, in my life as it is in
heaven. Only then will you be able to heal, overcome, obtain
deliverance, and move forward towards the abundant life God
has prepared for you, lacking nothing.

Prayer

God thank You for being the great architect of my life, for
knowing the plans that You have for me. You said that every
single one of my steps were ordered by You. Help me to accept
the things that I cannot change, but to align myself with Your
purpose for my life and move towards victory in Your name. Give
me the strength to endure the crushing. Give me peace as I travel
through every storm of my life, knowing that you are right here
with me. Holy Spirit comfort me! well up on the inside of me so
that there is room for nothing more! Help me to surrender to
your will, so that Your kingdom will come, and Your will be done
in my life as it is in heaven. I bless You and thank You for
knowing me before I was even conceived. Thank You for the

*plans that You have for me, even when I do not see the way. Heal me, deliver me, set me free from every mindset that will try to keep me bound. Your word says the mind governed by the flesh is death, but the mind governed by Your spirit is life and peace (**Romans 8:6**...so I speak peace right now, in the name of Jesus. Thank you for always hearing my prayers in Jesus' name. Amen*

Prayer SEVEN

God thank You for this day and for the opportunity to come before Your throne and speak to You. Thank You for always surrounding me with Your love, grace and mercy; for allowing Your angels to encamp around me, to watch over and protect me from all things seen and unseen. Thank You for who You are in the earth and in my life. Thank You for always being an ever-present help in my time of trouble and for giving me the capacity to persevere through every storm and trial that I may face in my life. You alone know what I am made of! Thank you, God, for placing everything that I need on the inside of me. When I forget, remind me who I am and of the strength that I hold within. Let me see myself the way You see me. I recognize that You would not give me these hurdles to cross if You didn't think I had the capacity to, or set a provision and a way to help me. You're an awesome God! You're the same God yesterday, today and forevermore. You don't lie. You keep your promises. Every trial and tribulation will be complete in time. This is only a test. This too shall pass. It is well. In Jesus name, Amen

<u>Barren but Not Abandoned</u>

My prayer for you is that you will seek the face of God, even in seasons of drought and barrenness in your life. The word of God informs us that, throughout life, we may embark on different journeys, experiencing various seasons. Seasons that we may not feel mentally or spiritually prepared for. However, the Author and Finisher of your faith knows what you are made of and has already equipped you for what lies ahead.

Ecclesiastes 3:1,14 NIV states *"there is a time for everything and a season for every activity under heaven. 14. I know that everything God does will endure forever; nothing can be added to it, and nothing taken from it. God does it so that men will revere Him."*

You may be thinking equipped how? What tools do I have that will help me get through this dry period of my life? I need God to come down here Himself and perform a miracle! God, are you listening? Hello God, it is me again, why aren't You answering me? Why have You forsaken me? Why have You left me barren?

Isaiah 54:1 NIV states *"Sing, O Barren woman you who never bore a child, burst into song, shout for joy, you who were never in labor; because more are the children of the desolate woman than of her who has a husband"* says the Lord.

God instructs us to sing, shout for joy, and burst into song even though we feel like a barren land. One of the greatest tools that God has given us in seasons of barrenness is praise and worship. Once we put on the garment of praise the atmosphere starts to shift. The Holy Spirit begins to overturn the soil of our rocky hearts and minds, to make them more malleable. The Spirit of the living God then begins to call forth the living water, that He placed on the inside of you, to cover the dry ground. The ground then begins to produce fruit that remains. As a result, the promises of God become evident in your life. As a result, morsels of God's kingdom are established on earth, as it is in heaven and God gets the glory and reverence that He deserves!

Isaiah 54:8 NIV states *"In a surge of anger I hid my face from you for a moment, but with everlasting kindness I will have compassion on you" says the Lord your Redeemer."*
This scripture gives us insight into why we may experience some of our dry seasons. Sometimes, God hides His face from us as He did the Israelites whenever they disobeyed Him and failed to walk in His ways. Other times God may be working some things out, in our favor and He's attempting to teach us how to activate the fruit of the Spirit, long suffering. **(Galatians 5:22-23 NKJV)**

Whatever God's reasoning is, have faith! God is with you! trust Him through the process. Allow His peace to overtake you, knowing that even though you feel barren, you are not abandoned. As His word says in **Isaiah 54:10 NIV** *"...Though the mountains be shaken and the hills be removed, yet my unfailing love for you will not be shaken nor my covenant of peace be removed", says the Lord who has compassion on you.*

Prayer

God, I give You all the glory and the honor that You deserve. I show reverence to You, knowing that my steps are ordered by You alone. I pray that You would continue to plow through the rocky soil of my heart and mind. Make my heart more malleable for You to shape and mold as You see fit. Let the walls that may have surrounded my heart fall like the walls of Jericho! so that I may walk in purpose and in abundance, as You have planned for me, before the foundations of the earth. Thank You for having compassion on me. Thank You for your peace that surpasses all understanding and for being the living water! Help me to stay planted by the stream, so that I have an endless supply to do the work You have called me to do, and I will forever give You the glory in Jesus' name. Amen.

Send the WORD

My prayer for you is that when you ask God for something, you believe it's already done! By doing so, you express your faith in Jesus Christ and walk in the authority that the Holy Spirit has given you. In **Matthew 8:7-8, 13 NKJV** *"And Jesus said to him I will come and heal him. The centurion answered and said, Lord, I am not worthy that You should come under my roof. But only speak a word, and my servant will be healed. Then Jesus said to the centurion, go your way and as you have believed so let it be done for you. And his servant was healed that same hour."* Jesus said the word and it was manifested. So, therefore just as Jesus spoke a word and it was manifested immediately. The word of God spoken over your life will be manifested now. The promises and prophecies will be manifested, but only in God's timing. How do we know that this is true? Reflect on your life and on the words, which God has spoken over it. Count the many blessings that have been manifested in your life and how your creator has rescued you from situations that were meant to destroy you. Sometimes we panic, because we react from a humanistic and not spiritual perspective, but God has always been and is still in control! As stated before, (**Matthew 8:23-27**) when Jesus and his disciples were in the boat in the middle of the storm, Jesus did not panic. He knew that at His command, at His word the storm would cease. Just remember when you go through the storms of life, and you do not know what the outcome will be; <u>do not panic</u>. Instead put your trust in God and in His word. In His timing, the storm will have no choice, but to cease! Place your focus on and faith in the Almighty God; knowing that if you ask, and it is His will, He will send His word and it shall be done at his command.

Kingdom Blessings,
Love Always,
Shareese

Shareese's 20 Declarations
with Supporting Scriptures
(Instructions: Make these declarations over your life by reading them out loud each day and watch the power of God change your life forever)

1. I decree and declare that I no longer have a carnal heart or mind, but a surrendered heart and mind in Christ Jesus. Amen. **Romans 8:6 NIV** *"The mind governed by the flesh is death, but the mind governed by the Spirit is life and peace"*

2. I decree and declare that I will walk in obedience to God. Obedience is better than sacrifice. Amen. **Psalm 128:1 NIV** *"Blessed are all who fear the Lord who walk in obedience to him"*

3. I decree and declare that my heart and mind will abide in thankfulness. In Jesus Name, Amen. **(1Thessalonians 5:18 NIV** *"give thanks in all circumstances for this is God's will for you in Christ Jesus."*

4. I decree and declare that from this day forward lack is not my portion. God has abundance designed for this house for His glory. Amen **Psalm 23:1 NIV** *"The Lord is my shepherd I lack nothing"* **Psalm 37:4 NIV** *"take delight in the Lord, and he will give you the desires of your heart"*

5. I decree and declare that my heart is malleable, and the heart of stone has been removed. The Lord will mold my heart into His own. In Jesus Name Amen. **Ezekiel 36:26 NIV** *"I will give you a new heart and put a new spirit in you; I will remove from you your heart of stone and give you a heart of flesh"*

6. I decree and declare that my children are blessed and covered by the blood of the Lamb. They will excel in all they do. In Jesus Name Amen. **Psalm 112:2 NIV** *"their children will be mighty in the land the generation of the upright will be blessed"*

7. I decree and declare that my wounded heart is healed by the blood of Jesus and no wicked seeds that have been planted will take root in the name of Jesus. My heart will only be malleable to the Holy Spirit. Amen **Psalm 30:2 NIV** *"Lord my God I called to you for help, and you healed me"*

8. I decree and declare that I have a quiet mind, ready to hear from God at all times, waiting for instruction under His wing. In Jesus Name Amen. **Isaiah 26:3 NIV** *"You will keep in perfect peace those whose minds are steadfast because they trust in you"*. **Romans 8:6 NIV** *"the mind governed by the flesh is death, but the mind governed by the spirit is life and peace"*

9. I decree and declare that God will carry me through every obstacle or challenging situation in my life. When I am weak, He is strong. He will restore my soul. In Jesus Name Amen. **Isaiah 12: 2 NIV** *"Surely God is my salvation I will trust and not be afraid the Lord the Lord himself is my strength and my defense he has become my salvation"* **Zechariah 4:6 NIV** *So He Said to Me, "This Is the Word of The Lord to Zerubbabel: Not by might nor by power, but by my Spirit says the Lord Almighty"*

10. I decree and declare that God's favor is over my life. His lovingkindness towards me and generations to come is my portion. In Jesus Name Amen. **Psalm 5:12 NIV** *"Surely Lord you bless the righteous you surround them with your favor as with a shield"*

11. I decree and declare that God walks with me daily, never leaving or forsaking me. He is a constant in my life, when no others are, in Jesus Name Amen. (Deuteronomy 31:6 NKJV *"Be strong and of good courage do not fear nor be afraid of them for the Lord your God He is the One who goes with you, He will not leave you nor forsake you"*

12. I decree and declare that I am whole. I am lacking nothing; all that God has placed in me will work for me. In Jesus Name, Amen. (Psalms 139:13 NKJV *"For You formed my inward parts. You covered me in my mother's womb. I will praise You, for I am fearfully and wonderfully made Marvelous are Your works, and that my soul knows very well"*

13. The Lord decreed "I am your father though others have abandoned you I will never leave or forsake you. I will walk by your side daily if you do My will for My people. Abide in Me and I will abide in you. Amen. 2 Corinthians 6:18 NIV *"AND I will be a Father to you, and you shall be My sons and daughters, says the Lord Almighty"*

14. I decree and declare that God knows me. I am precious in His sight, and he knows the very number of hairs on my head. He is my Father, and I am His daughter. Amen. John 3:16 NKJV *"For God so loved the world that He gave his only begotten son, that whoever believes in Him shall not perish, but have everlasting life.* Psalm 23:6 NIV *"surely your goodness and love will follow me all the days of my life and I will dwell in the house of the Lord forever"*

15. I decree and declare that I am healed and restored in the name of Jesus, who is able to heal every soul wound. Amen (Matthew 9:22 NIV *"Jesus turned and saw her "take heart daughter", He said, "your faith has healed you" and the woman was healed at that moment"*

16. I decree and declare that no evil shall befall me or my family. No plan, trap, or snare will prosper. In Jesus Name, Amen. Isaiah 54:17 NKJV *"No weapon formed against you shall prosper and every tongue which rises against you in judgment you shall condemn, this is the heritage of the servants of the Lord and their righteousness is from Me says the Lord"*

17. I decree and declare that I rest under the wing of the Almighty and I am planted next to streams of living water, so that I may bear fruit in my due season. In Jesus Name, Amen. Jeremiah 17:7 NKJV *"Blessed is the man who trusts in the Lord and whose hope is the Lord. For he shall be like a tree planted by the waters, which spreads out its roots by the river and will not fear when heat comes, but its leaf will be green and will not be anxious in the year of drought, nor will cease from yielding fruit"*

18. I decree and declare that I am healed. Sickness does not belong to me, because by His stripes I am healed. In Jesus Name, Amen. Isaiah 53:5 NKJV *"But He was wounded for our transgressions, He was bruised for our iniquities, the chastisement for our peace was upon Him and by His stripes we are healed"*

19. I decree and declare that the Holy Spirit is my comforter and will help me to push through any pain presented to me in my lifetime. In Jesus Name, Amen. John 14:26 NKJV *"But the Helper the Holy Spirit, whom*

the Father will send in My name, He will teach you all things and bring to your remembrance all things that I said to you. Peace, I leave with you My peace I give to you; not as the world gives do I give to you. Let not your heart be troubled neither let it be afraid"

20. **I decree and declare that I am a vessel to be used as He sees fit, for the Glory and the KINGDOM of God. In Jesus Name, Amen. John 15:16 NKJV** *"You did not choose me, but I chose you and appointed you, so that you might go and bear fruit, and that your fruit should remain, that whatever you ask the Father in my name He may give you"*

LIFE SCRIPTURES from SHAREESE BRITTON-AHORLU

- **Philippians 4:6-7 NKJV** *"Be anxious for nothing, but in everything, by prayer and supplication, with Thanksgiving, let your requests be made known to God; and the peace of God, which surpasses all understanding, will guard you hearts and minds through Christ Jesus"*

- **Romans 8:28 NKJV** *"And we know that all things work together for good to those who love God, to those who are called according to His purpose"*

- **Romans 8:30 NKJV** *"Moreover whom He Predestined these He also called; whom He called, these he also Justified; and whom He justified, these He also glorified"*

Prayer EIGHT

Conclusion

Spirit of the Living God, thank You for Your faithfulness and for being an ever-present help in the midst of trouble. Thank You for allowing me to accomplish things during my lifetime that I felt unprepared, unqualified and not called to do. It was only by Your grace, continual instruction and my obedience to Your Holy Spirit that the vision You gave me was manifested. Continue to order my steps, as I travel this path You have paved specifically for me. Allow Your word to be a lamp unto my feet and a light unto my path, as written in Psalm119:105. Let everything be for your Glory! Every accolade, accomplishment, award and every win here on earth must be for the Glory of God to be established. I declare that You are still moving, still working miracles on my behalf, still present, still relevant and life could not be breathed without You today or forevermore. Oh Lord, when I feel hopeless, remind me that by praying through my light afflictions, little morsels of hope will arise from Your Holy Spirit, to sustain me and be my daily bread.

In Jesus Name, Amen.

About the Author

Shareese Britton-Ahorlu has been serving God in various capacities for the past 26 years, by volunteering, community service and mentoring. She is a graduate of Rutgers University Class of 2002, with a Bachelor of Arts in Sociology, minoring in Religion. She pursued her degree with the goal of attaining a Masters in Divinity, intent on becoming a hospital Chaplain,

however, God had other plans! Shareese became God's chaplain when she later obtained a Bachelor of Science in Nursing, at Chamberlain University. She eventually found herself ministering to her patients, their families and colleagues. Shareese has served as a Registered Nurse, specializing in Critical Care/Trauma for 10 years, in the Emergency Department and currently practices Telehealth Nursing. Shareese has been a devoted wife, to her wonderful spouse Patrick Ahorlu, for over 22 years. She is also the mother to their three beautiful daughters, the eldest 22- and 14-year-old twins. Shareese was also a contributor to The Well Christian Newsletter, where her devotions have been featured each month. She believes in the power of prayer, love, hope and exercising faith, in an effort to impact the lives of everyone she encounters for God's glory.

59738560R00059